1 Robert Mazzocco, *Trader*
2 Cynthia Macdonald, *(W)holes*
3 Thomas Rabbitt, *The Booth Interstate*
4 Edward Hirsch, *For the Sleepwalkers*
5 Marie Ponsot, *Admit Impediment*
6 Brad Leithauser, *Hundreds of Fireflies*
7 Katha Pollitt, *Antarctic Traveller*
8 Nicholas Christopher, *On Tour with Rita*
9 Amy Clampitt, *The Kingfisher*
10 Alan Williamson, *Presence*
11 Stephen Sandy, *Riding to Greylock*
12 Pamela White Hadas, *Beside Herself*
13 Sharon Olds, *The Dead and the Living*
14 Peter Klappert, *The Idiot Princess of the Last Dynasty*
15 Mary Jo Salter, *Henry Purcell in Japan*
16 Norman Williams, *The Unlovely Child*
17 Marilyn Hacker, *Assumptions*
18 Amy Clampitt, *What the Light Was Like*
19 Cynthia Macdonald, *Alternate Means of Transport*
20 Brad Leithauser, *Cats of the Temple*
21 Edward Hirsch, *Wild Gratitude*
22 Brooks Haxton, *Dominion*
23 Mary Swander, *Driving the Body Back*
24 Thomas Lynch, *Skating with Heather Grace*
25 Sharon Olds, *The Gold Cell*
26 Amy Clampitt, *Archaic Figure*

ARCHAIC FIGURE

ARCHAIC FIGURE

poems by

AMY CLAMPITT

Alfred A. Knopf   New York   1987

THIS IS A BORZOI BOOK
PUBLISHED BY ALFRED A. KNOPF, INC.

Published in the United States by Alfred A. Knopf, Inc., New York,
and simultaneously in Canada by Random House of Canada Limited, Toronto.
Distributed by Random House, Inc., New York.

Owing to limitations of space, all acknowledgments for permission to
reprint previously published material are on page 113.

Library of Congress Cataloging-in-Publication Data
Clampitt, Amy.
Archaic figure.
I. Title.
PS3553.L23A89   1987   811'.54   86–46004
ISBN 0–394–55919–3
ISBN 0–394–75090–X (pbk.)

Manufactured in the United States of America
First Edition

For Peter Kybart, Howard Moss,
and Mary Jo Salter

The ancient consciousness of women, charged with suffering and sensibility, and for so many ages dumb, seems, in them, to have brimmed and overflowed . . .

VIRGINIA WOOLF, *The Common Reader*, on the heroines of George Eliot

CONTENTS

HELLAS

ARCHAIC FIGURE

Headless in East Berlin, no goddess
but a named mere girl (Ornithe, "Little Bird")
out of the rubble, six centuries underneath
     the plinth of what we quaintly call

Our Time, informs the foaming underside
of linden boulevards in bloom, sweet hide
laid open onto—sterile as an operating table,
     past the closed incision of the Wall—

the treeless reach of Alexanderplatz,
paved counterpart of the interior flatland,
halfway across the globe, we'd left behind:
     projection, factor, yield, the quantifiable

latitude; malls, runways, blacktop; tressed
cornsilk and alfalfa, drawn milk of the humdrum
nurture there were those of us who ran away from
     toward another, earlier, bonier

one, another middle of the earth, yearned-
for stepmotherland of Hölderlin and Goethe:
sunlight and grief, the cypress and the
     crucifix, the vivid poverty

of terraced slopes, of bread, wine, olives,
fig and pomegranate shade we stumbled into,
strolling the sad northern drizzle, in
     the uprooted Turks' quasi-bazaar,

as here, among uprooted artifacts, we've come
upon this shape's just-lifted pleats, her
chitoned stillness the cold chrism of a time
that saw—or so to us it seems—

with unexampled clarity to the black core
of what we are, of everything we were to be,
have since become. Who stands there headless.
Barbar, she would have called us all.

THE OLIVE GROVES OF THASOS

Thronging the warped treadmill
of antiquity, the silver-polled
assemblies, knothole-
tunneled, generations-old

abeyances, posthumous postures
and contortions of a common
weathering, their burled stupor
pierced and cloven

by fierce threnodies of
daybreak, penetrable,
root-cooled in dazzlements
of unquarried marble,

these wards of turbulence
beneath the shaken
shrines of the acropolis,
delivering a gray-green

annual glut of worry-
beads that blacken
in October, after the summer
people have all gone,

when from the villages along
the shore, where in the evenings
we watched the fishing
boats go out in strings

of three, in trinities,
from each of whose sterns
there bloomed a mimic
trinity of lanterns,

linked in a ring, as
darkness fell, to frame
a single, cyclic reënactment
of the timeless; and from

the plane-tree-dimmed, cool-
all-summer refuge
of hill villages above the
tideline of gray foliage;

from the middle villages
the buses pass through, their
hens, their dust and oleanders,
their voluble cafés no more

than islets in the vast,
single surf of olive
groves that circumscribe,
that are the chief live-

lihood and artifact of
Thasos—the whole populace
turns out, with tarpaulins and
poles, to bring in the harvest

of these trees: of this time-gnarled
community of elders—so many-
shaped, so warped, so densely
frugal, so graceful a company,

what more can we say, we who have
seen the summer boats go out,
tasted the dark honey, and savored
the oil-steeped, black, half-bitter fruit?

ANO PRINIOS

Transport was what we'd come in search of.
A hill village where no bus goes—
we caught a lift there in a pickup truck,
hopped down onto cobblestones. Dank plane trees,
root, branch and foliage, engulfed the square.
The mountain slope behind spoke, murmurous,
in tongues of torrents. In what was actually
someone's living room, a small bar at the back,
two men sat by the window, drinking coffee.
We asked for ouzo. Olives on a bed of herbs
came with it, and feta, freshly made.
What next? Conversation halted, stumbling,
drew repeated blanks. The woman of the house
sat half-retired, hands busy, needle-glint
releasing a slow rill of thread lace.
What it was for—a tablecloth, a baby's
christening robe perhaps—I tried to ask,
she tried to tell me, but the filament fell short.
The plane trees dripped. The old man,
the proprietor, moved in and out. A course
we hadn't asked for—two fishes, mountain trout
they must have been, served on a single plate—
was set between us: seasoned with leeks,
I could not guess what else, the ridged
flesh firm and delicate.
Later, as I came from the latrine,
the old man, intercepting, showed me
the rooms we might have slept in—hangings
vivid over whitewash, the blankets rough.
A disappointed avarice—how could we, savoring
a poverty rarer than any opulence, begin
to grasp how dear our fickle custom was?—
gloomed, hurtful as a bruise, on

our departure: the rooted and the footloose
each looking past the other, for something missed.
A scruple over how to deal with matters so
fundamental, and so unhandsome, restrained me,
for two years and more, from writing
of what happened in between: how happiness
asperged, redeemed, made the occasion
briefly articulate. One of the coffee-drinkers,
having vanished, came back in. He brought,
dripping as from a fountain, a branch just severed
from some fruit tree, loaded with drupes
that were, though still green, delectable.
Turning to the woman, I asked what
they were called in Greek. She answered,
"Damaskēno." Damson, damask, damascene:
the word hung, still hangs there,
glistening among its cognates.

TEMPE IN THE RAIN

What leaf-fringed legend haunts
this sodden loess of picnics,
sardine-tin litter dripped on
by unmythic fig and laurel—
what latterday pursuits,
      what struggle

to escape the tourist traps,
what souvenir-stall
indignities beside the
footbridge, what coffee bar
depopulated by a sudden
      summer downpour?

To this running anachronism,
the giggling, gray-green
roar that fills a gorge
(sweet Thames! run softly)
old books refer to as the
      vale of Tempe,

the tributaries writhe,
sidle, and defy connection
with the roadside spring, high
up, at which two days ago the
bus made an unscheduled
      stop (we

all got out, washed fruit, filled
bottles, drank from our hands,
found a marsh-marigold in
bloom) or with, above the plain
of Thessaly (Peneus shimmering
        like the Python

Apollo slew, and having slain,
fled here to undo the pollution)
the crazy pinnacles of silt
compacted, cracked open, rain-
and-wind-sanded, where hermit
        monks hole up in

precarious balconies aswarm with
reptilian slitherings, with
gilding, martyrdoms and demons,
with the bong of bells to deafen
and the smell of flame-warmed
        beeswax to sweeten

a side trip Spenser never
contemplated; nor did Keats,
on whose account I've just
jumped off the bus, in this
unseasonable summer rain, to
        find no trace

here of Apollo in pursuit,
mad for the green, leaf-
slippery virginity of Daphne,
but rather, in a hollow under
Mount Olympus' obliviously
        pagan shoulder,

this shrine warmed by a
fragrant sweat of brown beeswax—
where, since some memorial
piety seems called for, before
the ikon of another virgin,
        I've lit a taper.

OLYMPIA

The marble stumps, the plundered archeology of games—
the foot race, the hippodrome, the chariot on the racetrack;
the fox-and-geese-track in the schoolyard snow; the footprints
of the weasel and the fleeing fieldmouse, the quick pickpocket,
dexterity of hand embellishing the margins of disorder;
Harpo Marx's scamp-as-saint, a voiceless kosher Mozart;

the katydid-faced TV hockey goalie, who never heard of Mozart,
all vicious equanimity on ice: what's to enjoy but games?
Baseball, weekend football orgies, a day off at the racetrack,
that spinoff of the heavy Greeks' reverberating footprints.
(What culture, pre- or post-gunpowder, spawned the pickpocket?)
Games, the last prop as stunned civility trips into disorder:

Berlin in '36, then Buchenwald's drill sergeants of disorder.
What's to be done, then, with the equanimity of Mozart?
Mandelstam and friends converting into chanting-games
the wording of a ration book, till the vagaries of the racetrack
ran him down: his widow gathering up the filched footprints
of his racing mind, raffish and incorrigible as a pickpocket.

When heavy breathing plays the superhero, the pickpocket
at his quick work acts the antihero—a slight disorder
in the bronze of monuments, like the dexterity of Mozart,
sick with overwork, converting even hackwork into games.
How far such insolent hilarity is from the racetrack
of dead earnest, bent on obliterating misplaced footprints!

The marble retrospect, the paleozoology of footprints
taken over by the guided tour, the masher, the pickpocket,
the frog-pond *brek-ek-ek-ex ko-ax ko-ax*, the slight disorder
of what's unplanned, ad hoc, or made up on the spot: Mozart
dashing off a bawdy letter, Mandelstam with *sotto voce* games
tweaking the management until it drove him off the racetrack.

The heavy Greeks were deadly serious about their racetrack.
Since Pelops won there by a trick, the solemn footprints
of mythology have not been done with boding. The pickpocket
and the masher remain the faithful guardians of disorder;
they keep their equanimity, although they never heard of Mozart.
A pest on heavy breathing! *À bas* civility! Long live the games!

THERMOPYLAE

Where the bay flashed, and an unrecorded number
of the Persian troops, whip-flicked into the spear-
clogged hourglass of the pass, were impaled and fell
screaming from the precipice to drown, the mirror

clogs: geography too gathers dust, though busloads
of us (sandaled Germans mostly), hankering for
an attar or a foothold, a principle that still
applies, a cruse of oil, a watershed no rain erodes,

find small inkling of what was staved off here,
or saved. A calcined stillness, beehives, oleanders,
polluted air, the hung crags livid; on the little hill
(beneath, the bay flashed as men fell and went under

screaming) where a stone lion once stood in honor
of that grade-school byword of a troop commander
Leonidas, we ponder a funneled-down inscription: Tell
them for whom we came to kill and were killed, stranger,

how brute beauty, valor, act, air, pride, plume here
buckling, guttered: closed in from behind, our spears
smashed, as, the last defenders of the pass, we fell,
we charged like tusked brutes and gnawed like bears.

LEAVING YÁNNINA

The lake like glass, like space
framed in a verdigris of reeds:
the arrow-pointed threadpulls
of small boats that scarcely
flaw the surface,
the mosque a floating
waterlily-garden of the air
upended on a minaret.
                        Last night
as, thrusting past the public square,
the strut of a platoon in khaki
cut through the burble and
meander of the *volta*,
the warm whiff, from
souvlaki stalls, of burning meat
took on a hint of carnage.
                        This morning
in the little archeological museum, time
lies still: the earrings,
the arrowpoints, the spearheads
no one will ever flee again
through time
or space: some latent source
stands open like a room.

DODONA: ASKED OF THE ORACLE

The female body, its creases and declivities
leading to the sacred opening, the hollow
whose precincts, here, neither seduce nor threaten:
bee-hum, birdsong, side-oats' leaning awns,
the blowing grasses (one vivid
lizard flickers on gray stone,
is gone); the drifting
down of poplars; harebells,
convolvulus. The triumph-song,
far off, of strutting cocks
no threat, merely ridiculous. Olympus
a mountain range away: huge valleys
charged with gargantuan
foreshadowings, new-minted
laser glints of force.
                    From such bluster
was this once a place of refuge? Before Dione,
the dim earlier consort, gave place
to bitchy Hera (who for her nagging
had, of course, good cause),
was there a season when
the unraised voice, attuned
to civic reticence by whisperings
among totemic oak leaves,
might gain a hearing?
                    Or did that wounded,
melismatic howl, heard now from
the taxicab cassette, or filtered
through the heat of the debate
above the tric-trac—whether
of shaman, priest, muezzin
or lying, half-self-deceived seducer—
countervail: this siren

tremor, male, ancient,
mindless, that raises
Armageddons from within the doddering
sheep run of politics—this echo
of recesses deeper, even, than
the archetypal cleft of sex?

❀

THE MIRROR OF

THE GORGON

. . . the myriad tribes of the dead came thronging up
with a wondrous cry, and pale fear seized me, lest august
Persephone might send forth upon me from out the
house of Hades the head of the Gorgon, that awful
monster.

The Odyssey, XI, 631–635
(translation by A. T. Murray)

MEDUSA

The tentacles, the brazen phiz whose glare
stands every fibril of the mind on end—
lust looked at backward as it were,
an antique scare tactic, either self-protection
or a libel on the sex whose periodic
blossom hangs its ungathered garland
from the horned clockwork of the moon:
as cause or consequence, or both, hysteric
symptoms no doubt figure here. She'd been
a beauty till Poseidon, in a flagrant
trespass, closed with her on Athena's temple floor.

The tide-rip torrents in the blood, the dark
gods not to be denied—or a mere indiscretion?
Athena had no time at all for talk like this.
The sea-god might be her old rival, but the woman
he'd gone to bed with was the one who paid.
A virginal revenge at one remove—there's none more
sordid or more apt to ramify, as this one did:
the fulgent tresses roiled to water-snake-
like writhe, and for long lashes'
come-hither flutterings, the stare
that hardens the psyche's soft parts to rock.

The female ogre, for the Puritan
revisionists who took her over, had a new
and siren sliminess. John Milton
put her at the gate of hell, *a woman to
the waist, and fair; but ended foul, in
many a scaly fold, voluminous and vast—*
whose name indeed was Sin. And in the den
of doctrine run amok, the armored glister

of a plodding Holiness revealed her
as likewise divided but, all told, *most*
loathsome, filthy, foul, and full of vile disdain.

The Gorgon, though, is no such Manichean tease,
no mantrap caterer of forbidden dishes,
whose lewd stews keep transgression warm.
The stinging jellyfish, the tubeworm,
the tunicate, the sea anemone's
whorled comb are privier to her mysteries:
her salts are cold, her home-
land Hyperborean (the realm that gave us
the Snow Queen and the English gentleman),
her mask the ravening aspect of the moon,
her theater a threshing floor that terror froze.

Terror of origins: the sea's heave, the cold mother
of us all; disdain of the allure that draws us in,
that stifles as it nurtures, that feeds on
what it feeds, on what it comforts, whether male
or female: ay, in the very tissue of desire
lodge viscid barbs that turn the blood to coral,
the heartbeat to a bed of silicates. What surgeon
can unthread those multiplicities of cause
of hurt from its effect; dislodge, spicule by spicule,
the fearful armories within; unclench the airless
petrifaction toward the core, the geode's rigor?

PERSEUS

His errand took him to the brink of Ragnarok,
past the last pillar of the charted world, where rain-
worn prototypes of animals and men,
extinct long since, preserved the evidence
of rookeries whose motive force went dark,
sealed shut by that grimace: eroded
stumps of horror antedating even
Odysseus, for whom the Gorgon's head
harrowed with unmanning fear the corridors
of Tartarus, that feeding trough of nightmares,
where every look breeds dread: unstared-down landmark,
last, first and most primitive of portents.

He came armed with an adamantine kris
Hermes had lent him, plus certain items gotten
(as so often happens when crusading zeal
sets forth) by means not over nice: prodigious
sandals' heavier-than-air device, the cowl
of a purloined intelligence, the pouch of blackmail
extorted from the Graeae, a triplet sisterhood
tied to an economy of scarcity (one tooth and one
eye among them, intercepted as they slid
from hand to hand); and above all indispensable,
the shield Athena gave, whose burnished metal
served as an intervening mirror of the Gorgon.

Like any other prospector for the hard,
the heavy, the hideously toxic,
he knew the risk he ran: he could not look
except at one remove at what he'd vowed to take
and hustle out: that head, struck
bleeding from its trunk, whose clotted
dreadlocks and gagged, staring scowl became

23

the badge and totem of what no one can
encounter and survive: among dredged glisten-
ings of seaweed, the unfledged millennium—
the branched, ineradicable stem of time,
whose cold coils wind about the moon's inexorable clock.

And even as he fled, the undiplomatic
pouchful safely stowed, two angry other
Gorgons in pursuit (as any Greek will caution,
mischiefs tend to come in triplicate),
the stem he'd lopped, already pregnant by Poseidon,
gave birth to Chrysaor, precocious warrior
whose cumbering falchion would overhang
the ungrazed field, the unturned furrow of the future,
and to unbridled Pegasus, the winged fraternal twin
who kicked at Helicon, and from whose hoofprint sprung
the mirror flash among the cromlechs—one wet
eyeblink in the antediluvial dark.

HIPPOCRENE

I came to the puddle. I could not cross it. Identity failed
me. We are nothing, I said, and fell.

VIRGINIA WOOLF, *The Waves*

The cold spring
of an intense depression,
moon-horror-struck posthumous
offspring of Medusa,
harbinger of going under,
of death by water.

Though above the pillars
of ruined Sounion the air
is calm, the white-lipped,
violet-hued flowerbed
of drowning, fraying
at the rim,

lies sleek with signals
of unbeing: the cold hoofprint's
doorway into nothing
metamorphosing from a
puddle in a courtyard,
the huge irruption

of blank seas the psyche
cannot cross: the terror-
twinning muse, the siren
and the solace: done and
undone by water—whether
beyond the stormy

Hebrides, the voyage
out, the long-looked-forward-to
excursion to the lighthouse:
the Ouse closing over;
a fin, far out. The waves
break on the shore.

ATHENA

Force of reason, who shut up the shrill
foul Furies in the dungeon of the Parthenon,
led whimpering to the cave they live in still,

beneath the rock your city foundered on:
who, equivocating, taught revenge to sing
(or seem to, or be about to) a kindlier tune:

mind that can make a scheme of anything—
a game, a grid, a system, a mere folder
in the universal file drawer: uncompromising

mediatrix, virgin married to the welfare
of the body politic: deific contradiction,
warbonnet-wearing olive-bearer, author

of the law's delays, you who as talisman
and totem still wear the aegis, baleful
with Medusa's scowl (though shrunken

and self-mummified, a Gorgon still): cool
guarantor of the averted look, the guide
of Perseus, who killed and could not kill

the thing he'd hounded to its source, the dread
thing-in-itself none can elude, whose counter-
feit we halfway hanker for: aware (gone mad

with clarity) we have invented all you stand for,
though we despise the artifice—a space to savor
horror, to pre-enact our own undoing in—
living, we stare into the mirror of the Gorgon.

THE NEREIDS OF SERIPHOS

... Here Perseus left Danaë, and when after a successful
voyage he returned with Medusa's head, and found King
Polydectes making love to Danaë, he forthwith turned
him and all the Seriphiotes into stones.

J. T. BENT, *The Cyclades* (1885)

Sealed up in fright, the wedding party turned
to rock: the way they used to tell it,
one look at whatever the eye-catching
widow's son had brought back from
whatever place he'd gone—out west,
or was it somewhere back east they said?—
had done it. But pin anybody down,
you find evasions, hearsay, a mere blur
of allegation.
       And as for all that
weathered-clean economy, that fluted-pillared,
clear-eyed residue of myth—listen a minute
to the nineteenth-century traveler: "Of
all the towns in the Greek islands, Seriphos
will remain fixed in my mind as the
most filthy. The main street is a sewer
into which all the offal is thrown, and
it is tenanted by countless pigs. . . ."
               The mire,
the stink of pigsties, of privies, of
the chamber pot upstairs, of soured milk,
mildew, kerosene, the purgatorial Lysol.
Yes. All this we know. Down there among
said-to-be-domesticated beasts—
the boar, the fenced-in bull, green drool
from bovine lips, green ooze of cowflops—
that we are animals, mire-born,

mud-cumbered, chilled and full of fear,
we know.
            "The houses opening upon
this street were black holes, where sat families
shivering around charcoal fires. . . ." The discomforts
of Seriphos or of my own New Providence
(so called, an act of piety and resolution),
the terrors everybody knows about
and no one speaks of: God. Dying.
Getting caught. The telephone at midnight.
Fire. Tornadoes.
            Horse Poseidon.
An old woman comes hobbling in, crossing herself
lest the stranger cast on her the evil eye.
His query has to do with certain
survivals of belief—in Nereids,
to be precise. Closing her eyes,
she groans, then mutters, "I know nothing."
It had all happened years ago, of course.
Michael Kapuzacharias had been digging
near the church (here once again she
vehemently crosses herself) on what
had been a very calm, still day,
when suddenly a whirlwind came. They found him
lying senseless, and in that state
carried him home to his family. Of course.
The nineteenth-century traveler evinces
no surprise. All one, those whirlwinds—
Nereids, Harpies, whatever, such as carried
off the daughter of Pandareus.
Of course.
            But in landlocked New Providence
(so called), a place of fright as yet

uncertified, Greek myth being merely
Guido Reni in a frame above the blackboard,
the elements are otherwise accounted for.
Thus, on the third day of June, 1860,
the meetinghouse was lifted from its foundation
by a wind wrapped in a cloud (as an eyewitness
by the name of A. M. Mulford would describe it)
of a dark purplish color, changing,
as it approached, to a white mist
so thick he could not see the fence
some thirty feet away. Whereupon (he wrote)
the wind began to blow with a fearful,
hollow, roaring sound . . .
                              A place of fright,
rebuilt with stained glass and a belfry, where
the sessions that, each Sunday morning, passed
for worship, were chilled still further
by the presence of a well-off farmer's wife,
witheringly millinered, gowned, beaded,
vitrified; but in whose Gorgon look
nobody chose to speak of having met with
the evil eye—or with anything more notable
than the fatuity of those who'd rise above
the herd. The mire. The torpor.
                              No Nereids.
No Gorgons, "monstrous females with huge teeth
like those of swine"—thus Bulfinch,
nineteenth-century burnisher of myth,
who mentions "an ingenious theory . . .
that the Gorgons and the Graeae were only
personifications of the terrors of the sea."
Only. *Only!* (Shipwreck. Fear death by water,
whirlwind, waterspout, tornado.) No Nereids.

No Harpies. Bulfinch recycled to a tedious,
sapless anthology. Guido Reni, master
of those who prettify, auroral in a frame
above the blackboard in fifth grade. No mire.
No stink. The pig-tusked Gorgon
decertified, sealed up in fright
of the unmentionable:
                    Cancer. The
lurid budding of the menses. Having
your underpants fall down in public.
The epidemic that strikes down the young
before the name of what it was is known.
Exposure. Rape. Abortion. The mute
gropings of the wedding night
locked up in fright. Fright
locked in for life. Mere allegation.
Headed west, they say. Or was it
east? Nobody knows the story.

SERIPHOS UNVISITED

The Nereids have departed. A century
of progress, as some once quaintly
termed it, has passed that island by.

Though, come summer, others of the Cyclades
will swarm with topless Nordic beauties,
Seriphos has still so few amenities,

is still so nil in terms of monuments,
the *Guide Bleu* hands it a two-sentence
detour (damaged frescoes). Poverty and silence,

rust stains, juttings of suicidal rock,
an anchorage too far off the beaten track,
according to Durrell. He sends us back

to old J. T. Bent, the classic indefatigable
traveler, who's told us everything we'll
ever know of pig-thronged, dank-hovel-

holed-up-in Seriphos, summer or winter.
For rural mid-America, the housing's better;
the price of pork is up, pigs grow fatter

faster, are still pigs. Against tornadoes, still
no remedy. Sundays, the tone in the split-level,
L-plan ranch-style shrine is newly evangelical.

What else is new? Psychoanalysis.
The crabgrass rootstocks of the middle class—
O thou great Sameness of our works and days!—

absorb the spread of a small, still conclusion:
progress, a century and more of it, has gotten
us nowhere. New world or old, beneath the skin

there's no true novelty. The fossil trait you
thought you'd shed looms in the rear-view
mirror. An unprecedented analgesic brew

dilutes the touted California honey.
Our meat is pulverized mythology. The
Nereids of consequence have passed us by.

PERSEUS AIRBORNE

... Thereafter, Perseus was driven by warring winds all
over the vast expanse of sky. . . . Three times he saw the
frozen north, three times, borne southwards, he beheld
the claws of the Crab. . . .

OVID, *Metamorphoses*, Book IV
(translated by Mary M. Innes)

What lay beyond those blowing beaches,
that heaving barrier, was still unmapped:
the wind-scoured moors of Patagonia,
the blizzard whiteouts of the Antarctic,

vast scarfed screechings at the center
of a Caribbean air mass; the norther,
the chinook, El Niño; gale force in wait,
the lurking possibility of wind shears:

even for a son of Zeus the Thunderer
(who'd impregnated his mother Danaë,
in a daring raid, with pollen-gold),
to be airborne entails a daunting,

a radical insouciance. The B-52s
panting in tandem, not-quite-new-fangled
coursers of the Sun, howl up from grasslands
that were terra incognita once: beyond

the last temptation, the untaken leap
they now rehearse, rehearse, rehearse.

ATLAS IMMOBILIZED

Hulk grown monumental with refusal,
intolerable landlock under the stars
he cannot shift, cannot rescind, cannot
look up into the cave of—

delirium, myopic rockface, the towering
quagmires of infinity
shrunk to a hairshirt—
what ultimatum

binds this certitude upon his back
that once set in place, nothing can alter?
Is even the moon's seeming to loiter,
a half-hearted voyeur,

mere robotry? The wedding party
garroted inside the skull, the
psyche's well-heeled, wall-
to-wall captivity,

the conversation pit a desert: airborne
murder overhead in squadroned
follicles, mad seed of the
purely theoretical,

orbiting as talks continue, with the usual
handwringing: thrones, dominations, powers
adhering to the same unshakable
proposition: nothing

truly is except what overcomes. No
rapprochement: the moon looks in,
moves off again: Orion's
mitered studs once more

abrade the hemisphere. Are all these
rigors fixed, the single step
untakable, the postures of the
conversation pit unfree

to bend, to make amends? Were all
that's still locked up in fright
to shriek, might not some warden, even
yet, unforge the key?

A GATHERING

OF SHADES

"I'm very brave, generally," he went on in a low voice: "only today I happen to have a headache."
Through the Looking Glass

GEORGE ELIOT COUNTRY

For Gordon Haight
(1901–1985)

From this Midland scene—glum slagheaps,
barge canals, gray sheep, the vivid overlap
of wheatfield and mustard hillside like
out-of-season sunshine, the crabbed silhouette
of oak trees (each joint a knot, each knot
a principled demurral—tough, arthritic, stubborn
as the character of her own father)—fame,
the accretion of a Pyrrhic happiness, had
exiled her to London, with its carriages
and calling cards, its screaming headaches.

Griff House—dear old Griff, she wistfully
apostrophized it—in those days still intact,
its secrets kept, has now been grafted to a
motel-cum-parking-lot beside the trunk road,
whose raw, ungainly seam of noise cuts through
the rainy solace of Griff Lane: birdsong,
coal smoke, the silvered powderings of
blackthorn, a flowering cherry tree's
chaste flare; the sludge-born, apoplectic
screech of jet aircraft tilting overhead.

The unmapped sources that still fed nostalgia
for a rural childhood survive the witherings
of retrospect: the look of brickyards,
stench of silk mills, scar of coal mines,
the knife of class distinction: wall-enclosed,
parkland-embosomed, green-lawned Arbury Hall,
fan-vaulting's stately fakeries, the jewel-
stomachered, authentic shock of Mary Fitton and

39

her ilk portrayed, the view of fishponds—school
and role model of landed-proprietary England.

Born in the year of Peterloo, George Eliot
had no illusions as to the expense of such
emoluments. Good society (she wrote), floated
on gossamer wings of light irony, required no less
than an entire, arduous national existence,
condensed into unfragrant, deafening factories,
cramped into mines, sweating at furnaces, or
scattered in lonely houses on the clayey or chalky
cornland . . . where Maggie Tulliver, despairing
of gentility, ran off to join the gypsies.

Violets still bloom beside the square-towered
parish church where Mary Anne was christened;
the gashed nave of Coventry fills up with rain
(another howling doodlebug of fright hurls itself
over); the church from which, refusing to commit
the fiction of a lost belief in One True Body,
she stayed away, upholds the fabric in which her
fictions, perdurable now, cohere like fact: Lydgate
still broods, Grandcourt still threatens, and
in Mrs. Transome disappointment turns to stone.

MEDUSA AT BROADSTAIRS

A seaside place so tranquil
her very mind might drift, grow indolent,
become a tidepool: the articulate spine,
its resolutions and attenuations—all
acquired at such a price—
sweetly let go.

This couldn't last, of course. It never did.

On Saturday the 10th, H.S. came down—
to whom she'd cheerfully agreed
(and let the fact be widely known)
that she was not attached.

No use. The unwanted love-child of a note
she evidently handed him survives. The stored-up
spikenard of ardor in its ungainly vessel—
whole forests of it, bending and shimmering—
again refused. Aged thirty-three
and still so quick to feel, so soon
a rigid gazingstock.

Night terrors. The huge claustrophobia of childhood
starting up again: the dried shriek,
the claw about the windpipe.

Medusa, whether stinging jelly with no backbone
or stare of fury petrified,
in wait: the obscure cold pool
where Hetty, unlikely early offspring of George Eliot—
mindless, adorable, the smoldering dark girl
who must, her fatuous ardor ditched,

be done away with—will not be brave enough
to drown herself, to have it over:

The motions of a little vessel without ballast
(she'd write): the horrors
of this cold, and darkness, and solitude,
out of all human reach, becoming greater
every minute . . . The bitter waters spread,
the Arthur Donnithornes, the Stephen Guests
ride by: John Chapman, Herbert Spencer:
"If you become attached to someone else"
(she ignominiously writes) "then I must die."

There will be more: the sudden cold
about the knees, the inundated threshold,
Maggie Tulliver awake, borne outward
by (recurring nightmare of her childhood)
the actual surge: the same dark girl
grown tall and mindful, whose excesses
must be done away with, drowned.

George Eliot is not yet, Hetty Sorel not yet,
nor Maggie Tulliver, except (If you
become attached to someone else . . .)
in aching embryo. Only
long-faced, brainy Marian, prone
to hysterics. Back in London,
the usual observances—four walls
closing in, headache that lasts an age—
are sure to follow.

HIGHGATE CEMETERY

Laid in unconsecrated ground, a scandal
still—note how good Gerard Hopkins
recoiled from what a queer, awkward girl,
frail-shouldered, massive, rickety,
volcanic, out of an unconsecrated
attachment, a marriage that was
no marriage (one would have added,
till opprobrium intervened, *but
something better*) to a pockmarked
lightweight of a drama critic,
saw blossom: this domestic improbability,
this moonflower: they were happy.

Happiness: *that*—as it always has been—
was the scandal. As for the uninhibited
pursuit of same, gone merrily
amok, by now, among the lit-up
purlieus of a game show (died
of a conniption, beaming): time
spared her that, though not the cold shoulder,
the raw east wind, fog, the roar that issues
from the other side of silence; not headache,
kidney stone, the ravages of cancer—or
of grief foreseen, met with, engulfed by,
just barely lived through.

Nature (she'd written, years before) *repairs
her ravages, but not all. The hills
underneath their green vestures bear
the marks of past rending.* Johnny Cross,
younger by two decades, a banker,
athletic, handsome, read Dante with her,

43

fell in love; repeatedly, distressingly,
spoke of marriage, was at last accepted.
Another scandal—in the eyes of devotees
who looked on marrying at all with horror
as for the breathing fishbowl of appearances.
Grotesque, my dear. An episode in Venice,
on their honeymoon (who knows what makes any
of us do what we do?) was somehow weathered.
Then, in six months, she was dead.

At Highgate, the day she was buried,
a cold rain fell, mixed with snow. Slush
underfoot. Mud tracked inside the chapel.
Her brother Isaac, more than twenty years estranged
(a ravage never healed), was there
among the mourners—hordes of them,
the weather notwithstanding. Edith Simcox,
crazed with devotion to this woman who'd been,
in her ill-favored way, so beautiful, arrived
with a nosegay of violets, wandered off distracted
into the dusk, came to herself finally
at a station she didn't recognize,
somewhere in Hampstead.

In rain-wet May, not quite a century later—
cow parsley head-high, the unkempt
walks a blur, faint drip of birdsong,
ivy taking over—the stone is hard to find.
Herbert Spencer, a creature of exemplary
good sense, however ill-equipped
for rapture, lies buried not far off,
his monumental neighbor a likeness

of Karl Marx, egregious in granite—
godfather of such looked-for victories
over incorrigible Nature, his memory red
with nosegays ribboned in Chinese.

MARGARET FULLER, 1847

In this her thirty-seventh year, the Italy
she'd discerned already smoldering,
through some queer geological contortion,
beneath a New World crust, abruptly ceased
to be a metaphor. She was in Rome,
and from her lodgings on the Corso
she watched as things began to happen:
the torchlit procession to the Quirinal,
the flung-out embrace of Pio Nono
from his balcony seeming (at least)
to give the upheaval in the streets his blessing.

By September, in Florence, in Milan,
more demonstrations: that second spring
she'd once despaired of, the kernel
lying dormant in the husk no longer,
the shattered chrysalis, the tidal
concourse in the streets and through the bloodstream
one and the same. Angelo Ossoli, whom
she'd met by chance—the faintly scandalous
perennial adventure that awaits a woman,
of whatever age or status, in such a place—
was now her lover. Without the cause he'd drawn

her into—a mutilated Italy made whole,
at peace within, left to itself at last,
the hated foreign uniforms gone home—
she'd once again have kept her head,
perhaps: remained unconscionably chaste,
seen the admirer she'd somehow led on
pull back bewildered as, her self-esteem
gone numb, she worked at being noble.
Not now. Not in this place. The furnace

that had scathed her solitude burned with the torches,
glowed in the votive banks lit by the faithful.

The two of them went frequently to Mass;
on long excursions into the countryside
inhaled the reek of grapes still on the vine,
observed the harvest. The violets and roses
that still bloomed made her bedroom sweet
all through November. "I have not been so well,"
she wrote her mother, "since I was a child, nor
so happy ever." *Nor so happy ever.* Short of money,
she lived now in one room, on fruit, bread,
a little wine; saw few acquaintances,
dissembled, as she'd so often done, even with those.

The mild days shrank. A season ended.
Nor so happy ever. In mid-December
a cold, steady rain began. Increasingly
the high-walled towers along the Corso
shut out the daylight. *Since I was a child*:
then there had been terror
in the night, as now: she'd wake
alone to find herself back in Nantasket,
where she'd dreamed her mother dead,
re-dreamed her best friend's body lying
on hard sand, until the waves reclaimed it,

drowned. Brave metaphor of tides became,
lodged in that sullen dark, a heaving
succubus of mud. The street-corner
flower vendors disappeared.
Lamplit all day, the stale cul-de-sac
she could not leave now stank of charcoal

and the chamber pot. Migraine, a vengeful
ever-since-childhood doppelgänger,
returned, with a new kind of nausea:
the body so little of her life had ever
found sweetness in, life for its own inexorable

purposes took over. "A strange lilting lean
old maid," Carlyle had called her—though
not nearly such a bore as he'd expected.
What would Carlyle, what would straitlaced
Horace Greeley, what would fastidious
Nathaniel Hawthorne, what would all Concord,
all New England and her own mother
say now? An actuality more fraught
than any nightmare: terrors of the sea,
of childbirth, the massive, slow,
unending heave of human trouble.

Injustice. Ridicule. What did she *do*?
it would be asked (as though that mattered).
Gave birth. Lived through a revolution.
Nursed its wounded. Saw it run aground.
Published a book or two.
And drowned.

GRASMERE

For Lois Squires

Rainstorms that blacken like a headache
where mosses thicken, and the mornings
smell of jonquils, the stillness
of hung fells thronged with the primaveral
noise of waterfalls—contentment
pours in spate from every slope; the lake fills,
the kingcups drown, and still it rains,
the sheep graze, their black lambs bounce
and skitter in the wet: such weather
one cannot say, here, why
one is still so happy.

Cannot say, except it's both so wild
and so tea-cozy cozy, so snugly
lush, so English.

A run-into-the-ground complacency nonetheless
is given pause here. At Dove Cottage
dark rooms bloom with coal fires; the backstairs
escape hatch into a precipitous small orchard
still opens; bedded cowslips, primroses,
fritillaries' checkered, upside-down
brown tulips still flourish where
the great man fled the neighbors:
a crank ("Ye torrents, with
your strong and constant voice, protest
the wrong," he cried—i.e., against the Kendal-
to-Windermere railway). By middle age a Tory,
a somewhat tedious egotist even (his wild
oats sown abroad) when young: "He cannot," his sister
had conceded, "be so pleasing as my

49

fondness makes him"—a coda
to the epistolary cry, "Oh Jane
the last time we were together he
won my affection . . ." What gives one
pause here—otherwise one might not
care, as somehow one does,
for William Wordsworth—
is Dorothy.

"Wednesday. . . . He read me his poem. After dinner
he made a pillow of my shoulder—I read to him
and my Beloved slept."

The upstairs bedroom where the roof leaked
and the chimney smoked, the cool buttery
where water runs, still voluble, under the flagstones;
the room she settled into after his marriage
to Mary Hutchinson, and shared with, as
the family grew, first one, then
two of the children; the newsprint
she papered it with for warmth (the circle
of domestic tranquillity cannot
guard her who sleeps single
from the Cumbrian cold) still legible:
such was the dreamed-of place, so long
too much to hope for. "It was in winter
(at Christmas) when he was last at Forncett,
and every day as soon as we rose from dinner
we used to pace the gravel in the Garden
till six o'clock." And this,
transcribed for Jane alone from
one of William's letters: "Oh, my dear, dear Sister
with what transport shall I again

meet you, with what rapture . . ." The orphan
dream they'd entertained, that she had named
The Day of My Felicity: to live
together under the same roof,
in the same house. Here,
at Dove Cottage.

"A quiet night. The fire flutters, and
the watch ticks. I hear nothing else
save the breathing of my Beloved . . ."

Spring, when it arrived again, would bring
birch foliage filmy as the bridal veil
she'd never wear; birds singing; the sacred stain
of bluebells on the hillsides; fiddleheads
uncoiling in the brakes, inside each coil
a spine of bronze, pristinely hoary;
male, clean-limbed ash trees whiskered
with a foam of pollen; bridelike
above White Moss Common, a lone wild cherry
candle-mirrored in the pewter of the lake.
On March 22nd—a rainy day, with William
very poorly—resolves were made
to settle matters with Annette, in France,
and that he should go to Mary. On the 27th,
after a day fraught with anxiety, a morning
of divine excitement: At breakfast
William wrote part of an ode. It was
the *Intimations*.

The day after, they took the excitement to Coleridge
at Keswick, arriving soaked to the skin. There, after dinner,
she had one of her headaches.

A bad one's ghastly worst, the packed ganglion's
black blood clot: The Day of My Felicity
curled up inside a single sac with its
perfidious twin, the neurasthenic
nineteenth-century housemate
and counterpart of William's incorrigibly
nervous stomach: "I do not know from what
cause it is," he wrote, "but during
the last three years I have never
had a pen in my hand five minutes
before my whole frame becomes a bundle
of uneasiness." To ail, here in this place,
this hollow formed as though to be the vessel
of contentment—of sweet mornings
smelling of jonquils, of tranquillity
at nightfall, of habitual strolls
along the lakeshore, among the bracken
the old, coiled-up agitation
glistening: birds singing, the greening
birches in their wedding veils,
the purple stain of bluebells:

attachment's uncut knot—so rich, so dark,
so dense a node the ache still bleeds,
still binds, but cannot speak.

COLEORTON

Again, at evening, the winter walks
supported on her brother's arm—not,
as at Forncett, snatched, fugitive,
but an entitlement, an earned dependency,
the welding of everything somehow since
lived through: her brother's wedding day,
those vows whose undertow was of such force
it laid her prostrate on an unfamiliar bed:
Mary, her sister now, delivered
of three babies—"all famous," declares
their father, who can be a wag, can
quite well write a letter when he chooses,
"for being exceedingly ill-managed":
sweet, stolid, vengeful Johnny; Dora,
a tireless chatterer; and poor Thomas, in
the midst of teething, who cries and cries:
three safe lyings-in, cut through by one
fearful bereavement: washed ashore
weeks after the *Abergavenny* foundered,
the body of John Wordsworth lies
in Wyke churchyard, on the Dorset coast. No stone
marks it. Two years will soon have passed.
They have not gone there. At Grasmere,
every gale that shudders in the chimneys
is his memorial—made the more poignant
by months, night after night, of worrying
over Coleridge.
           Whom they await here,
while the forebodings thicken: worse,
yes, worse even than their brother's shipwreck
(though that has left her shrunken, pitiful
and old at thirty-five—"They tell me,"
she writes, "I have never looked so well

in my life. This *I* do not believe"), the shock
of Coleridge returned from Malta,
bloated, despondent, sodden. The ruined
landmarks of dependency mere breath,
oneself a leaf, a weak vine lifted, dandled,
dropped: the poet's whimper of "There is
a change, and I am poor": to be deprived
for life of what not even she, whose shoulder
he'd made a pillow of, after the labor,
the lying-in of genius: a genius unstable,
large, of little note, sneered at
by the reviewers: deprived of what
not even she can any longer offer! This it is
that throbs between them like an abscess
as they pace, at evening, below
Coleorton Hall.
                    His altered look:
the gray-eyed luminary of the day,
not quite a decade since he first,
leaping that stream, had been admitted
to the startled core of their attachment,
now sunk in fat: the stillborn squalor
of their late reunion, the meeting he'd
repeatedly eluded, more charged with dread
than the stark loss of John, so wholly
to be depended on, so blameless.
Without blame, only an overweening,
hurt solicitude, they wait for him
to end the maundering requitals, the
evasions of an ending, and quit the ruin
that is his marriage; while the hum
and tremor of a blander tie, the bondage
of a new endearment, is entered on

with Lady Beaumont, whom they're beholden to
for this lent space, these walks at evening,
the unobstructed sunsets of which at Grasmere,
"shut up as we are in our deep valley,
we have but a glimpse. . . . On Wednesday evening,
my Brother and I walked backwards and forwards
under the trees . . . until the sky
was all over gloomy, and two lights
(we supposed from coal-pits) were left to shine . . .
I have kept back from speaking of Coleridge,
for what can I say? . . ."
                                    They wait.
The Poem of Her Brother's Life, that portico
to the unbuilt cathedral of his mind—"divine"
had been the word set down by Coleridge himself
that day when, listening high among the tarns,
he'd felt the lintel of it soar, heard an
entire design reverberate—that prelude
to a greater undertaking waits. Turned
landscape architect meanwhile, her brother
charts for his patron a winter garden
"which shall present no image of chillness,
decay or desolation when the face of nature
everywhere is cold, decayed or desolate. . . .
We never" (he continues) "pass in our evening walk
the cluster of holly bushes . . . but we unsettle
a number of small birds which have taken shelter
there. . . . The whole Bush seems aflutter. . . ."
His mind wanders backward into summer, to a time
when what had seemed the idyl of dependency
rushed into blossom: "I never saw so beautiful
a shrub as one tall holly . . . near a house
we occupied" (another house not theirs—

55

how many since those winter walks at Forncett,
the scene of their resolve to live together
under one roof!) "in Somersetshire:
it was attired with woodbine, and upon
the very tip of the topmost bough
'that looked out at the sky' " (a tremor
here—fallacious pathos of the one
red leaf, last of its clan, that dances
topmost) "was one large honeysuckle flower,
like a star. . . ."
                    They wait. Together,
as the older stars come into bloom
above the coal-pits, they look up
and feel the prospect darken.

RYDAL MOUNT

"Now, I must tell you of our grandeur,"
she'd written. "We are going to have
a *Turkey*!!! carpet in the dining room . . .
You stare . . . 'Are they changed, are they
setting up for fine Folk. . . ?' " Yes,

they were changed. One year had seen
comic, crippled Catharine, aged three,
and Thomas, of whom much had been expected,
both laid in Grasmere churchyard; then
their father, already gray and elderly

at just past forty, set in a position:
Distributor of Stamps for Westmorland,
canvasser for the Lowthers, who all but
owned Penrith ("Sad, sad, sad," radical
John Keats would mutter, passing through).

Soon she'd be caught up with him in all
the brouhaha of a bought election. Yes,
there had been a change: De Quincey, so
lately of their household, so innocently
besotted with Catharine, married now

to opium and the simple girl he'd gotten
a bastard by. "Ruined," D. pronounced. And
paid no more visits. From Dove Cottage—
the talk there, the incandescent silences
beside the fire ("I hear nothing else save

the breathing of my Beloved")—indeed
there was a change. Her brother wrote
now, grandly, of Mutability, of outward
forms (unspecified) that melt away
like hoarfrost. Surprised by joy (he wrote),

he'd turned to share the transport—turned
to whom but Catharine, with a sublimity
he could no more come down from than she,
poor mite, in life could walk upright. Aloft
at such an eminence, he'd grown more craggy;

nobody argued with him; much wifely tact
was spent, a whole household of amanuenses
circled him on tiptoe. Reputation sealed in,
spicule by spicule, the old sore wounds—
grief, ridicule, the worm of conscience:

Annette and Caroline, the larger work undone.
Word came that Coleridge was dead. "A long
sit with knitting on my knee," his sister
noted in her diary. Words for the chill
he felt came more slowly: *power frozen*

at its marvellous source . . . Our haughty
life is crowned with darkness, like London
with its own black wreath. There had been
great alteration: that was the year
his sister—the ruin of her youth beset

by mass defections from within the body,
the firebrand of her old vivacity half-
quenched, a hutch of glowworms—in flight
from grandeur, vicissitude, fine Folk,
took refuge in the nunnery of madness.

Fits of verse, poured out from memory.
Churchwardens mocked. Unseemly noises.
Outbursts. Children and strangers kept away.
Small, shrunken, wild-eyed, she'd command
whoever came into the room to stir the fire.

There would be remissions. "News—news,"
she'd write. "I must seek for news. My
own thoughts are a wilderness . . . The
laburnum with its naked seedpods shivers. . . ."
"Stir the fire!" Her brother, poet laureate

since Southey died, obeys her, sits here
with her, watching: a doddering pair, like
gypsies camping out, the way they'd camped
one night at Tintern, the untended grandeurs
of a time gone dim gone dim behind them.

THE ODESSA STEPS

Old lady with the pince-nez whirling,
there on the steps, to meet the bayonets—
would she, given, in that twinkling of an
eyeglass smashed, the option, have gone home
and shut the door before the trouble started,
preferring ikon and samovar to all those changes,
promises of an upheaval far too heady
to be kept: or would she have declared
that to have died there, where the action was,
inhaling an ozone that only in transit
tastes like splendor, was to have been lucky?

Dark mother of an ailing boy, aghast
as at a long atrocity exhumed, the damp
of catacombs still on it: shade
from the same cleft that opened, halfway
around the world, on an Ohio hillside
where shots were fired—a kneeling,
incredulous dark girl's mouthed O
the Soviet cinema's unconscious ape:
a runaway, picked up two years after
for loitering with intent, her moment of
pure grief, fame's discard, an unhoused ruin.

Wheels of the upended baby carriage
flailing, there on the steps, a visionary
metaphor derailed: where are the wheels
Ezekiel saw ablaze, where are the eyes,
the voice, the noise of many waters?
Who looked for openings, for signs
of a new age beginning, finds instead

a shutdown: these gray lives' torpor,
the labor gangs, the litter on the freeway,
fleered-at shapes of windmills gone rotten,
the Satanic millwheels still grinding.

AN ANATOMY OF MIGRAINE

In memory of Annette Leo

I

Inquire what consciousness is made of
with Galen, with Leonardo, Leeuwenhoek
or Dr. Tulp, and you find two hemispheres,
    a walnut in a bath of humors,

a skullcapped wreath of arteries, a weft
of fibrous thoroughfares along the walls
of Plato's cave, the cave walls of Lascaux:
    those shambling herds, this hollow

populous with fissures, declivities,
arboreal thicketings, with pairings
and degrees, this fist-sized flutter,
    mirror-lake of matter,

seat of dolor and jubilee, the law of Moses
and the giggling underneath the bedclothes,
of Bedlam and the Coronation Anthem—all
    these shut up in a nutshell.

Go back, step past the nadir of whatever
happened to divide our reckoning, a fraction
of an anti-millennium, a millennium and more
    ago, and hear Hippocrates declare

the brain is double. Since then, as to
where, in these paired hemispheres, the self—
with its precarious sense of *I am I*,
    with its extremes of possibility—

resides, we've come no nearer than
Descartes, who thought he'd found it in
the pineal teardrop. (Now no one's sure
     what that gland is for.)

Inquire what consciousness is made of
of Simone Weil, and she answers: Pain.
The drag of gravity. The sledge of time.
     A wretchedness no system

can redeem, extreme affliction that
destroys the *I*; nothing is worse, she
wrote. And knew whereof she wrote, who'd
     drudged, with an ineptitude

only the saints would find becoming,
in a Renault assembly line; had seen
the waste, how small the profit, how
     many suffer and learn nothing, how,

as Kate Croy observed (and chose accordingly),
deprivation made people selfish, left them
robbed of the last rags of character,
     preyed and put upon, enmired in rancor.

She'd seen, was not immune, had been there;
had her own cliffs of fall within the skull:
headache, driven by whose cringing thud
     she'd scrupulously noted

a craven urge within herself to cause
someone, anyone, to suffer likewise.
Is the mind divided, as Hippocrates
    declared the brain is?

Did she invite in what all but unhinged her?
She'd known well-being, however threaded
with crevasses; been witness to the white
    stars' stillness overhead, the white

drift of petals from the apple trees: such
tranquil spanglings of the retina of time,
she could not doubt the universe
    is full, that splendors

of entity, of grace past meeting face
to face, project, each one, its fearful
opposite, its double—as each electron
    in the universe its Manichaean

anti-particle: in every molecule of
every nerve cell, such forces within
forces within forces, the marvel
    is that anyone is ever well,

that consciousness is ever other than
a frazzled buzz, one long sick headache.
My father never gave the name of migraine
    to that locked-in retribution

of the self against—against who knows
what or whom? Fenced brutes, barbed wire
and rawhide, fear of a father's anger,
    mere heredity? His father,

to a grandchild seemingly so mild, so
equable, had labored, I would one day
learn, through that same territory:
    days of headache, nights so worry-

racked he thought his mind would go.
Heredity: finally, in a little memoir
impelled by painful rectitude, he'd
    set down how dread

of what had made him made *his* father
by temper hard: got out of wedlock,
the old conundrum—*Who am I? where did
    I come from?*—twice riddled,

learning whose bastard he was, he'd
manfully assumed that surname. Stirred
or unstirred, the generations' cesspool
    fills; the circle of the wrathful,

ventilated, usurps the crawl space:
all Hell's hand-me-downs hung from
the spindle of Necessity, each sprung-
    from-two, spun-out-of-nothing

being crying from within, *I, I,*
while time that bears the thinking
being toward what it cannot bear
   impales it here.

2

Here is impaled—hinge, mirror-image,
cleft, and crossing-place—the hard
world-knot of entity, the One not one
   at all but contradiction,

Nohow and Contrariwise, chiasmus through
the looking-glass: fraternal inter-
twinings, at the very core a battle;
   so the neurobiological

dilemma of the paired, the hemispheric,
re-ramifies—bright, dark; left, right;
right, wrong—and so euphoria gives way to
   spleen, its obverse, as though

the cosmos repented of itself, of all those
promises, all those placebos: the sun-flooded
square, stone blossoming, each canvas seen as
   a live aperture, a space

to step into; then the usual consequence,
of waking to another migraine: three days
in a darkened room, the drastic easement
   of ergot, derivative of poisoned

66

rye long known to midwives, proscribed for
her too fragile bloodways. (Lift the hem
of medicine, and you discover torture
    and placebo twinned, still there.)

No cure. This happened, was set down.
I read the manuscript amazed. We hadn't met.
Letters had been exchanged, her driven,
    bannered penmanship an

army out of *Alexander Nevsky*—the whips,
the wolves, the keening steppes, the Russian
mother-lap her history had been torn from.
    One day a parcel came,

impeccably hand-wrapped, inside it an
uncrafted something—three sea-winnowed
sandstones, a wave-buffed driftwood elbow—
    from the beach at Malibu.

I blushed, both flattered and adroitly
remonstrated with: the manuscript (so many
women writing books, their scripts unread,
    still hoping for some recognition!) I'd

said I'd look at not yet opened. I opened
it that day—though not before an ounce
of Maine-coast beach glass had been
    wrapped and sent, transcon-

tinental reciprocity—and read it through.
The migraine on the day she was to fly
to Italy, a frame and a foreshadow
    of that volatile chiaroscuro,

a life repeatedly, strenuously, just barely
put back in order—that migraine (*You too!*)
set her instantly, for me, with an elite
    vised by the same splenic coronet:

Dorothy Wordsworth, George Eliot, Margaret
Fuller, Marx, Freud, Tolstoy, Chopin, Lewis
Carroll, Simone Weil, Virginia Woolf:
    a gathering of shades, of

forebears and best friends who'd all gone
to that hard school. Since Homer peered
at Tartarus, we've looked into a gazetteer-
    authenticated Hell, a place for

meeting with—for hearing yet again the
voices of—the dead. The cosmos, looped with
bigfoot odysseys set down in moon dust, now
    gives it no place but in the hollow

of the skull: that Amazon where no explorer
goes except on hands and knees, the strait
last entrance to the fields of asphodel
    where, say, Simone Weil

and Virginia Woolf might meet and find no distance,
after all, in what they'd finally perceived—
what the latter wrote of as " 'reality' . . . beside
    which nothing matters"; she who'd,

at moments, bridged the mind's crevasse: "Lying
in bed, mad, & seeing the sunlight quivering, like
gold water, on the wall, I've heard the voices of the
    dead here, and felt, through it all, exquisitely

happy." Anny, friend by mail, what I would give
for time to talk of this! We met just once; at ease
at once, walked barefoot on the sands at Malibu,
    the blue air that afternoon, by

some semantic miracle, angelic; picked up stones,
observed the dolphins. A last letter, in that script
her unemphatic beauty stanched without a trace.
    Then, in a hand I did not recognize—

cramped, small, precise—one from the husband
who'd survived her: dead in her sleep. No
warning. But she'd known, had written of, in
    one half-retracted note, a premonition.

I miss her. Though our two lives just touched,
the torn fabric of some not-yet-imagined
prospect hangs there, streamered, splendid,
    vague: well-being rainbowed

over a lagoon of dark: all that I'm even
halfway sure of marked by that interior cleft
(black, white; sweet, sour; adazzle, dim), I
   live with shades of possibility,

with strangers, friends I never spoke to, with
the voices of the dead, the sunlight like gold
water on the wall—electron-charged, precarious—
   all tenuously made of consciousness.

ALICE

For an Oxford don, doomed during term to sit
night after night at the high table,
the pardon of a little girl afloat
on an unstygian Thames. No Sibyl
gloomed or ranted at the rabbithole
she entered by—a time-obsessed fussbudget
of a rabbit her Virgil—into the hell
her elders were so grandly glum about.

Persephone and Beatrice among the shades,
she showed the monstrous region underground
for what he'd always thought it was:
the screeching shams, the burbled pieties,
the flummoxes and trapdoors of the mind:
all Oxford flattened to a pack of cards.

ATTACHMENTS, LINKS,

DEPENDENCIES

LONDON INSIDE AND OUTSIDE

Looked back on happily, the ivy-hung,
back-wall-embowered garden of our
pied-à-terre and domicile in Chelsea
seems oddly like some dream of living
halfway down the well that sheltered
Charles Dodgson's Elsie, Lacie
and Tillie—with those geraniums
in urns, that lily-of-the-valley
bed not quite in bloom, those churring
ringdoves, those thrushes murderously
foraging for earthworms: an exterior
so self-contained, a view so inward
that though at night we'd note
faint window-glimmerings eclipsed by ivy,
we seemed to have no neighbors either
to spy on or be spied on by.

Those strolls at dusk, the sidewalks
puddled underfoot, the streetlamps
an aloof processional (a footfall
once or twice, then silence)
at the hour not of the pulling down
of shades but rather of the drawing
in of curtains on their rods, with
an occasional small, to-be-savored
lapse—the glimpse in solitude
of the young woman meditatively
taking off her coat: or of
the table laid, the TV
in the dining room tuned to the news,
a South-Sea-bubble porthole open
on the mysteries of domicile,
of anchorage, of inside-outside!

75

The night we took the Underground
to Covent Garden, we found the foyer
at the opera a roofed-in waterfall
of crystal, the staircase we sat on
at the interval to eat our ices
carpet-luscious (even to the shod
sole) as a bed of crimson mosses,
the rose-red lampshades erotic
as hothouse hibiscus. Floated
overhead, a firmament of gilt
and turquoise; as that goes dim,
beneath the royal monogram the bell jar
of illusion lifts, and yet again
we're inside-outside: Norina's
rooftop vista (the duenna
furiously knitting) of a hot-bright
Bay of Naples. In the obscurity
of our neck-craning balcony, we
snuggled undetected. Outside there waited
a shivering, rain-speckled exodus among
dark gardens of the inevitable
umbrellas going up.

BABEL ABOARD THE HELLAS
INTERNATIONAL EXPRESS

Border halt, an hour out of Saloniki.
Washrooms already filthy. Corridor
a frisson of peaked caps, red-seaweed
postage-stamp outlandishnesses at a
standoff. *Gastarbeiter* bound for Munich

in a second-class couchette: sad Greek
whose wife is sick (he tells us in
sepulchral German), who can't stop smoking—
a brown, brown-suited man, his runneled
face a map of nicotine. Slaves of caffeine,

we hop down, throng the last-chance café (none
aboard the train, none in Yugoslavia. No
food either. Warned, we've brought aboard
bread, cheese, wine, olives, peaches), stoke
ourselves with swarthy oversweetened coffee

while brown man lays in his own supply
of—what? It's yogurt: five, six, seven
plastic-lidded tublets' curded slime. He
stacks them (and we shudder) on the filthy
floor. We cut cheese. He smokes. He can't

stop smoking. By designation the compartment
is *Nicht Raucher,* 'Απαγορεύεται τὸ Κάπνισμα.
Useless to complain. We're sorry for him.
And anyhow there's a fourth occupant, a
brown man too, who seems inscrutable (he might

be Greek, or might not be) and who, without
apology, murkily, incessantly *ist auch ein
Raucher*—though mainly in the corridor.
Dusk. We're moving. We've crossed the border.
We halt again. We're sots and thralls

of Babel and demography. New ghouls
have come aboard. We scare each other,
telling of papers gone astray. We're passing
through a gorge. The lockstep trudge brings in
new hues, new snarls of peaked-cap seaweed,

old mores, old anxieties: our pasteboard
vitals handed over, peered into, returned or
not returned, repeatedly. It's dark outside.
Glimpses of halted freight cars. Someone
flourishing a flashlight walks the track, to spy

out what spies? what contraband? It's coffee,
someone says. They opened up somebody's suitcase
back there, found it packed with kilo bagfuls. Took
them all. Detained the passenger. We're pouring
wine. Trudge, trudge. Visa control again:

passports one by one are handed back. Mine
not among them. Why? Where is it? Ghoul
shrugs. Trapdoor opening—fright, indignation,
fury, sputtered futile questions. Gallantry
between us: "I'll stay with you." "No,

no. You go on to Munich. You know
you must." I don't believe a word of this, of
course. I take a Miltown. Reiterated gusts
of asking why, dire glee of strangers. Next,
Skopje. I'm being brave. I'm not being brave, I am

in fact behaving childishly. Washroom
so filthy you can't squat. No drinking
water either. Worse: it now turns out
I'm not a martyr. The latest peaked-cap
wearer fingers my shoulder bag. I look

and squirm: It's there. Who put it back?
No way of knowing. "I do feel such a fool.
You won't tell anyone? I'll never live it down."
"It might have been some trick of theirs,"
you say, still gallant. Maybe. I doubt it.

The Skopje passengers flood in. "Komplett!
Komplett!" Our brown companions fend them off.
We settle onto our couchettes. Wake in Belgrade.
No coffee. Hawkers of pasty, tasteless pastries.
New hordes crowd aboard. It's Sunday morning.

"Komplett! Komplett!" All Yugoslavia is traveling,
won't be kept out. The kerchiefed proletariat
from Istanbul, who got on back at Nis, may
be deterred, but not the middle class.
A couple and their little boy have joined us—

sad, tight-garbed, stodgy-prosperous.
Their little boy is blind. Their burden,
shared, is our affliction. Salamander-pale,
he sways, croons, laughs convulsively,
is told to hush; whimpers, subsides again

to sea-cave solitudes we can't envision.
At Zagreb they leave us. The crowds are worse.
"Komplett! Komplett!" No use. Disconsolate
brown man whose wife is sick climbs back
onto top berth to sleep—the one last solace.

His untouched yogurt has begun to spill. A mess.
The washrooms are by now a costive-making,
hopeless *cauchemar*. The Serbs, Slovenes,
Croatians, Bosnians, Albanians, who knows what
else, who swarm the corridors, are civil,

appeal to reason, persist, at last prevail.
Stout ruddy woman; lean, fair-haired, ruddy man;
two small dark nondescripts; one human barrel,
chalk-stripe-tailored, curly-brilliantined,
Lech Walesa–mustachioed, jovial: with these,

till Munich, we're to share what space there is.
They speak some common dialect, we're not
sure which. A bag of prunes is passed.
We offer olives. The conversation grows
expansive: we listen in on every syllable,

uncomprehending, entranced. A bottle
circulates: I hesitate, see what it is,
and sip. Stupendous. Not to be missed,
this brew. It burns, it blazes. Anecdote
evolves, extends, achieves a high adagio,

grows confidential, ends in guffaws. O
for a muse of slivovitz, that fiery booze,
to celebrate this Babel, this untranslatable
divertimento all the way to Munich,
aboard a filthy train that's four hours late!

SALONIKI

For Ben Sonnenberg

Rust-hulled freighters in
a violet bay; lean cats
that slink, finches
that sing and sing;
sunflowers' exotic
hunchback candlesticks

beside the hovel of an
early Christian church,
later a mosque: Byzantium
profaned shored up again,
Ezekiel bird-caged in prophetic
fire's faint shreds, a relic
of the arson of the Turks.

Apricots, sweet cherries,
hazelnuts—what's not
for sale here? Bird-market
cheepings, the interminable
murmurings of doves and politics;
under the arcades of Odos
Aristotelous, the plastic
of a hundred thousand fakes.

VENICE REVISITED

While the Frenchmen and Flemings abandoned themselves in a frenzy of wholesale destruction, the Venetians
kept their heads. They knew beauty when they saw it.
JOHN JULIUS NORWICH, *A History of Venice*

I

Guise and disguise, the mirrorings and masquerades.
brocaded wallowings, ascensions, levitations:
glimmering interiors, beaked motley; the hide-
and-seek of Tintoretto and Carpaccio. From within
walled gardens' green enclave, a blackbird's warble—
gypsy non sequitur out of root-cumbered
terra firma, a mainland stepped from
to this shored-up barge, this Bucintoro
of mirage, of artifice. Outside the noon-dim
dining room, the all-these-years-uninterrupted
sloshing of canals; bagged refuse, ungathered
filth; the unfed cats, still waiting.
                                    To breathe again
the faint stink of this place I had not thought to
revisit in this life; to catch, through shutters
half-latched for the siesta, the same glimpse
of a young girl's laundry—a glimpse half-
preternatural, like an encounter with some
evidence of resurrection: re-entering, to swim
above the mild tumuli of San Marco,
that last surreal upwelling of Byzantium,
is also to disinter the vertigo
of the homesteader's wife who, numb
in the face of the undisguised
prospect of the place she'd come to, drove
a post into the yard outside the sodhouse
to have something, she said, to look at.

2

The place they'd come to—treeless, its sole prospect
the watery skin-scurf of reedbeds, of mudflats
cowering shivering in the dark or sweltering
at noon, no place to hide from vertigo—was no
less desolate. They lived at first
dispersed, in dens of osier and wattle,
hemmed by no familiar dolomite, no tree-blurred
watershed to lift the eyes to—the lagoon
a wan presentiment of the great basin's
vastness—a place for a homesteader's wife
to drift and drown, or else to settle and
grow stolid as a driven post in.
                              Postpiles driven
into the muck of the lagoon—a million-plus of them,
a thousand-plus times over—would one day undergird
the multiplicity of domes, arcades, façades
of variegated marble, stilts for the stupendous
masquerade of history: the Bucintoro
with the Doge afloat, rowed to the cheering
of lubricious throngs, the whimpering
of lutes: a stage set above the windings
of these onetime sloughs, the hidden
thoroughfares obscure and treacherous
as the dim wagon tracks the homesteaders
would inevitably follow into the disguiseless
grassland, the desolation of
the place they'd come to.

3

Magnificence of guise and disguise, of the given
and the taken: that a body thought to be
that of Saint Mark—Evangelist, witness to
the crime that had then given birth to faith,
subscriber to the possibility of resurrection—
had been brought here from somewhere, is
believed to be historical. Whether the box
they brought it in—the filched cadaver,
the purported-to-be-sacred relic—in fact contained
merely another masquerade, has long since
ceased to matter. Maskers, lovers of shows,
of music, looters who knew beauty when
they saw it, who (while others rampaged,
raped, or merely smashed) made off with
the famous four bronze horses, and much else,
they did know beauty: give them
at least that credit.
                    What stolen relics,
sacred or bogus, what odor of sanctity
or of corruption, would the descendants
of the homesteader's wife who drove
that post to keep herself from going
mad, bring home, to furnish and inform
the likewise unhandsomely acquired
terrain she'd come to? What mainland—
if there is a mainland any more for any
emigré's descendants to return to—
can they claim? What's to be said for
their, for our own faltering empire,
our most unserene republic, other
than that while crusaders of our own

rampaged in Asia, one set foot also
on the maskless, indubitable
wasteland of the moon?

MAN FEEDING PIGEONS

It was the form of the thing, the unmanaged
symmetry of it, of whatever it was
he convoked as he knelt on the sidewalk
and laid out from his unfastened briefcase
a benefaction of breadcrumbs—this band

arriving of the unhoused and opportune
we have always with us, composing
as they fed, heads together, wing tip
and tail edge serrated like chicory
(that heavenly weed, that cerulean

commoner of waste places), but with a
glimmer in it, as though the winged
beings of all the mosaics of Ravenna
had gotten the message somehow and come
flying in to rejoin the living: plump-

contoured as the pomegranates and pears
in a Della Robbia holiday wreath that had
put on the bloom, once again, of the soon
to perish, to begin to decay, to re-enter
that dance of freewheeling dervishes,

the breakdown of order: it was the form
of the thing, if a thing is what it was,
and not the merest wisp of a part of
a process—this unraveling inkling
of the envisioned, of states of being

past alteration, of all that we've
never quite imagined except by way of
the body: the winged proclamations,
the wheelings, the stairways, the
vast, concentric, paradisal rose.

PROGRESS AT BUILDING SITE
WITH (FEWER) PIGEONS

Visitors, a lost last remnant,
to the pilgrim shrine
of something neither we
nor they know what
to make of,
they hang in, homing,
above the pit a swiveling
derrick gangles out of—
at its foot, far down,
a yellow scutterer
of an earth mover

engaged in trading
with a red, caterpillar-
pedestaled steam shovel
at street level,
crawfuls (gouged,
precarious, self-undermining)
of the very precipice
it's perched on—such
large gobblings
and regurgitations
miming a

by now obliterated
memory of being fed,
eons ago, atop
some window ledge,
the ghostly lost
escarpment of an
extinguished other country. See

how the winged vagrants
still hover, haunting
the laddered cage's
gusty interstices

like the question no one
poses, as to what we're,
any of us, doing
here: what is this
elbowed, unsheltering,
obtrusively
concatenated fiefdom
we poor, cliff-dwelling
pseudo-pioneers
have somehow
blundered into?

MIDSUMMER IN
THE BLUEBERRY BARRENS

Away from the shore, the roads dwindle and lose themselves
among the blueberry barrens. The soil is tired;
what little there was of it in these upland
watersheds wore out years ago.

This is a region rich only in lilacs. Vacancy
stares from the half-drawn blind of an
upstairs window; the porch sags; the abandoned van,
its wheels gone, rusts underneath the evergreens.

The children are already too listless, their elders
too much defeated, to think of pomp or high jinks
on midsummer eve; instead of pagan bonfires
there will be some drunkenness, some wives will be beaten.

In *bella Firenze*, on the feast of San Giovanni Battista,
young men of good family, in biretta and doublet, the velvets
of a day more ceremonious, if not necessarily happier
or more just, ride toward the Duomo. "*Lei piace?*"
someone, smiling, inquires of a tourist.

And the tourist, here in the city of Savonarola,
is pleased, if a trifle bewildered. John the Baptist
came crying repentance, to prepare the way for simplicity,
for such as are capable of sorrow. To do so, then as now,
was to be labeled a common scold or a public nuisance.

Along the shore, away from the blueberry barrens,
the larger houses are being aired,
the clay courts are being rolled for the tennis matches,
the pleasure craft, their sails furled neatly,
rock at their moorings.

Life is good, here by the shore; simply to look at the ocean
is tranquillizing, a cure for anxiety. At St. John's
by-the-Sea, where the sacrament of the Lord's Supper
every first Sunday is one of the pleasures,
the name-day of the Baptist is absently remembered.

"Prepare the way," he came crying, but the world
was not ready for him. A princess danced
with his head on a salver. Here by the shore,
away from the blueberry barrens, we are still not ready
for such singleness, for so much sorrow.

TIDEWATER WINTER

After the treetop-filtered
tangerine of dawn,
the zenith's frescoed-by-
Tiepolo cerulean,

an afterglow of thinnest
autumn-crocus-tinted
porcelain, looked up into
through seedpod-

skeletal crape myrtles:
the light for days
replayed itself in some such
phased transparencies,

then dimmed one morning
to a daylong monochrome
of snow, and on the next to
ground fog's numb,

windless whiteness,
muting the waterways,
muffling the cypresses'
pendulous residues

of other weathers, the
dried chandeliers
of tulip trees, the sweet gums'
dangled pomanders,

muffling the lumberyards,
pine plantations, warehouses,
the hunched or gangling
shapes of enterprises

either with or without
proclaiming patronyms
(here's Nabisco, here's Lone Star
Cement); the loading platforms,

watertanks and power lines. Along
the borders of the cypress-knee-
filled, thawed or frozen
inlets of the Chickahominy,

the locomotive sways and sings
the long single
song, the brayed, incessant,
searching syllable

of passing through, of
always moving on.
Tidewater left behind, by Richmond
the ground fog's gone.

RUNES, BLURS, SAP RISING

In January, shed twigs of hemlock
leave their runic offprint of an
autograph on thawing snowbanks

whose meltwaters go down loquacious
in torques, in curdlings, cadenzas
by the earful. Today, out walking

among the evergreens—toplofty
taperers, cones, puptents—I've come
upon the guarded quiddity of how a

beech tree signs itself, in punctual
lifts, in skaterly glissandos;
how the alder neatly, minutely

rounds off each period with a
catkin's knob; and just now, in an
embrasure of the understory, this

deciduous tightrope processional,
these leaf-buds like a thing afire:
looked at up close, their quasi-

bronze a finely grooved, a paired
and pointed Asian gesture, self-
effacingly inscrutable. What

will it be? A viburnum, green
wings erupting, then a foaming
torque of bloom? No telling—

other than, come April, all
linear pronouncements will be
awash with leaf-blood's delible,
    blurred, tidal signature.

CONTINENTAL DRIFT

As from a freckling on
the paving to a mottling
to a merging blur, the rain
invents a continent of
inundation: or
as the minute, sharp, shining
leaf buds at each
twig-tip of the
linden in the garden
open from translucent
dappling to an overlapping
gloom of green, of
summer shadow
that will yellow

and unroof, leaf
by down-drifting leaf,
into a fallen continent,
a sediment of leaf mold,
the seethe of entity
undoes what's done,
the sieve unselves,
the drift within
proceeds from dark
to dark, from rift to
rift, from mooring
to castoff
off uncharted
continental shelves

THE WATERFALL

Orb-weaver shivering
among the filaments: how many
fibers generated from within
transect the air?

How many hirsute, sightless
gropings anchor
these redwood trees, suffuse
the flowery traceries

of the oxalis? The veining
in this hand, these
eyeballs, the circuitous
and scintillating

leap within the brain—
the synapse,
the waterfall, the black-
thread mane of fern

beside it—all, all
suspend, here:
everywhere, existences
hang by a hair

A HERMIT THRUSH

Nothing's certain.   Crossing, on this longest day,
the low-tide-uncovered isthmus, scrambling up
the scree-slope of what at high tide
will be again an island,

to where, a decade since well-being staked
the slender, unpremeditated claim that brings us
back, year after year, lugging the
makings of another picnic—

the cucumber sandwiches, the sea-air-sanctified
fig newtons—there's no knowing what the slamming
seas, the gales of yet another winter
may have done. Still there,

the gust-beleaguered single spruce tree,
the ant-thronged, root-snelled moss, grass
and clover tuffet underneath it,
edges frazzled raw

but, like our own prolonged attachment, holding.
Whatever moral lesson might commend itself,
there's no use drawing one,
there's nothing here

to seize on as exemplifying any so-called virtue
(holding on despite adversity, perhaps) or
any no-more-than-human tendency—
stubborn adherence, say,

to a wholly wrongheaded tenet. Though to
hold on in any case means taking less and less
for granted, some few things seem nearly
certain, as that the longest day

will come again, will seem to hold its breath,
the months-long exhalation of diminishment
again begin. Last night you woke me
for a look at Jupiter,

that vast cinder wheeled unblinking
in a bath of galaxies. Watching, we traveled
toward an apprehension all but impossible
to be held onto—

that no point is fixed, that there's no foothold
but roams untethered save by such snells,
such sailor's knots, such stays
and guy wires as are

mainly of our own devising. From such an
empyrean, aloof seraphic mentors urge us
to look down on all attachment,
on any bonding, as

in the end untenable. Base as it is, from
year to year the earth's sore surface
mends and rebinds itself, however
and as best it can, with

thread of cinquefoil, tendril of the magenta
beach pea, trammel of bramble; with easings,
mulchings, fragrances, the gray-green
bayberry's cool poultice—

and what can't finally be mended, the salt air
proceeds to buff and rarefy: the lopped carnage
of the seaward spruce clump weathers
lustrous, to wood-silver.

Little is certain, other than the tide that
circumscribes us, that still sets its term
to every picnic—today we stayed too long
again, and got our feet wet—

and all attachment may prove at best, perhaps,
a broken, a much-mended thing. Watching
the longest day take cover under
a monk's-cowl overcast,

with thunder, rain and wind, then waiting,
we drop everything to listen as a
hermit thrush distills its fragmentary,
hesitant, in the end

unbroken music. From what source (beyond us, or
the wells within?) such links perceived arrive—
diminished sequences so uninsistingly
not even human—there's

hardly a vocabulary left to wonder, uncertain
as we are of so much in this existence, this
botched, cumbersome, much-mended,
not unsatisfactory thing.

NOTES

From E. Homann-Wedeking, *The Art of Archaic Greece*, translated by J. R. Foster (Greystone Press, 1968, pp. 96–97, 98): "There [on the island of Samos], about 560 B.C., a donor erected in the sanctuary of Hera a long base on which six marble statues stood side by side. . . . All the figures had names inscribed on them. The artist, Geneleos by name, also inscribed his own name. . . . The execution of each individual figure is unsurpassable. The statue of Ornithe can serve as an example. The special delicacy of the surface texture lies in the quite shallow modelling and the tender, tranquil play of the folds of drapery. . . . The garment is brought to life by the quiet gesture of the right hand lightly catching up the material. Statues like that of Ornithe were the prototypes which inspired the sculptors of the other regions of Greece to produce similar works. The clothing alone would show that Ionia was the source of these figures. There the oldest of them are dressed in the chiton, a tunic-like garment made of thin, delicate material. . . ."

From Fernand Braudel, *The Mediterranean*, Volume I (Harper & Row, 1975, p. 241): "The truth is that the Mediterranean has struggled against a fundamental poverty, aggravated but not entirely accounted for by circumstances. It affords a precarious living, in spite of its apparent or real advantages. It is easy to be deceived by its famous charm and beauty. Even as experienced a geographer as Philippson was dazzled, like all visitors from the North, by the sun, the colours, the warmth, the winter roses, the early fruits. Goethe at Vicenza was captivated by the popular street life with its open stalls and dreamed of taking back home with him a little of the magic air of the South. Even when one is aware of the reality it is difficult to associate these scenes of brilliance and gaiety with images of misery and physical hardship."

The title is the name of a mountain village in Greece.

"TEMPE IN THE RAIN"

From *The New Larousse Encyclopedia of Mythology* (Prometheus Press, 1968, pp. 95–96): "The mariner who sailed into the gulf of Therme (today the gulf of Salonica) would feel himself filled with religious awe when he perceived against the hard blue line of sky the lofty profile of Mount Olympus. Everything concurred to reveal to him the fearful majesty of the gods. In the first place he had no doubt that Olympus was the highest mountain in the world. Then he would remember that the narrow Vale of Tempe, which separates Olympus from Ossa and cradles under its willows and plane-trees the peaceful stream of Peneus, had been hollowed out by Zeus during his struggle with the Titans."

"OLYMPIA"

From *Hope Against Hope*, by Nadezhda Mandelstam (Atheneum, 1970, p. 120): "In the summer of 1935 M. was granted the favor of receiving an identity paper valid for three months, accompanied by a residence permit for the same period. This made our lives much easier. . . . People who live in countries without identity papers will never know what joys can be extracted from these magic little documents. In the days when M.'s were still a precious novelty, the gift of a benevolent fate, Yakhontov came to Voronezh on tour. In Moscow M. and he had amused themselves by reading from the ration books which were used in the excellent store open only to writers. M. refers to this in his poem 'The Apartment': 'I read ration books and listen to hempen speeches.' Now Yakhontov and M. did the same thing with their identity papers, and it must be said that the effect was even more depressing. In the ration book they read off the coupons solo and in chorus: 'Milk, milk, milk . . . cheese, meat. . . .' When Yakhontov read from the identity papers, he managed to put ominous and menacing inflections in his voice: 'Basis on which issued . . . issued . . . by whom issued . . . special entries . . . permit to reside, permit to reside, permit to reside. . . .' "

From Book Seven of the *Histories* of Herodotus, translated by Aubrey de Selincourt (Penguin Books, 1954, p. 493): "There was a bitter struggle over the body of Leonidas; four times the Greeks drove the enemy off, and at last by their valour succeeded in dragging it away. So it went on, until the fresh troops with Ephialtes were close at hand; and then, when the Greeks knew that they had come, the character of the fighting changed. They withdrew again into the narrow neck of the pass, behind the walls, and took up a position in a single compact body—all except the Thebans—on the little hill at the entrance to the pass, where the stone lion in memory of Leonidas stands to-day. Here they resisted to the last, with their swords, if they had them, and, if not, with their hands and teeth, until the Persians, coming on from the front over the ruins of the wall and closing in from behind, finally overwhelmed them."

"LEAVING YÁNNINA"

Yánnina: a lakeside town in northern Greece. *Volta*: the evening promenade that is a custom in Mediterranean countries.

"DODONA: ASKED OF THE ORACLE"

From *The New Larousse Encyclopedia of Mythology*, p. 98: "The most famous sanctuary of Zeus was that of Dodona, in Epirus. It was also the oldest, dating back to the Pelasgians. People came there from all parts of Greece to consult the oracle of a sacred oak whose rustling and murmurs were regarded as the words of Zeus himself. On the origin of this oracle Herodotus, who claims to have heard it from the lips of the priestesses of Dodona, says: 'Two black doves flew from Thebes in Egypt, one to Libya and the other to Dodona. The latter, alighting in an oak tree, began to speak in a human voice and to ask that an oracle of Zeus should be founded in this place. The people of Dodona believed that they had received an order coming from the gods, and on the dove's advice founded the oracle.' ... The goddess Dione ... was venerated at Dodona at the side of Zeus, here taking over the role of Hera."

"MEDUSA"

On the Gorgons, from *A Handbook of Greek Mythology*, by H. J. Rose (Dutton, 1959, pp. 29–30): "With regard to the Gorgons, it has been rightly pointed out, for instance by Miss Harrison, that we hear of the head of the Gorgon before anything is told us of the Gorgon herself. The kernel of the myth is, that there existed sometime and somewhere a creature of aspect so terrible that those who saw her turned at once into stone. . . . Once started on its way, this idea would naturally blend with the widespread superstition, common in both ancient and modern Greece, of the evil eye. . . . The older Greek art . . . shows a horrible, grinning head, with flat nose, lolling tongue, and staring eyes, sometimes adding a striding, winged body. With this the descriptions of poets later than Homer correspond. In particular several passages give the Gorgons serpents in their hair or girdles, with other monstrous features. . . . As a result of the Greek hatred of ugliness, or possibly to avoid representing Poseidon as being in love with anything so misshapen as the traditional Gorgon, later art shows Medusa as a beautiful woman, from about 300 B.C. on with a look of terror or pain about the eyes."

"HIPPOCRENE"

From *The Diary of Virginia Woolf*, edited by Anne Olivier Bell, Volume Three (Harcourt Brace Jovanovich, 1980, p. 113): "Thursday 30 September. I wished to add some remarks to this, on the mystical side of this solitude; how it is not oneself but something in the universe that one's left with. It is this that is frightening & exciting in the midst of my profound gloom, depression, boredom, whatever it is: One sees a fin passing far out. What image can I reach to convey what I mean? Really there is none I think. The interesting thing is that in all my feeling & thinking I have never come up against this before. Life is, soberly & accurately, the oddest affair; has in it the essence of reality. I used to feel this as a child—couldn't step across a puddle once I remember, for thinking, how strange—what am I? &c. But by writing I dont reach anything. All I mean to make is a note of a curious state of mind. I hazard the guess that it may be the impulse behind another book. . . ."

"ATHENA"

ae'gis, e'gis, n. [L. from Gr. *aigis*, a goatskin, from *aix, aigos*, a goat.]
1. in Greek mythology, a shield or breastplate; originally applied to
the shield worn by Jupiter. In later times, a part of the armor of Pallas
Athena, appearing as a kind of breastplate covered with metal scales and
the head of the Gorgon Medusa, and fringed with serpents.
—Webster's Unabridged Dictionary

"THE NEREIDS OF SERIPHOS"

James Theodore Bent's classic travel book, *The Cyclades: Or Life
Among the Insular Greeks*, was published by Longmans, Green and
Company, London, in 1885.

A. M. Mulford's account of the tornado he witnessed appears in the
History of Hardin County, Iowa, published in 1883.

"SERIPHOS UNVISITED"

What little Lawrence Durrell has to say of Seriphos is to be found on
p. 254 of his *The Greek Islands* (Viking-Penguin, 1978).

"ATLAS IMMOBILIZED"

The story of how, after refusing hospitality to Perseus, the giant Atlas
was transformed into a mountain, is told in the *Metamorphoses* of Ovid,
Book IV.

"MEDUSA AT BROADSTAIRS"

Selections from George Eliot's Letters, edited by Gordon S. Haight
(Yale University Press, 1985, pp. 100–102), contains the texts of two
letters from Marian Evans to Herbert Spencer dating to July 1852. In
the first she wrote of her state of mind at Broadstairs, "I think of retiring

from the world, like old Weller, if my good landlady will accept me as a tenant all the year round. I fancy I should soon be on an equality, in point of sensibility, with the star-fish and sea-egg—perhaps you will wickedly say, I certainly want little of being a *Medusa. . . .*"

From *Adam Bede* (Everyman Edition, reprinted 1973, p. 369): "It was the same rounded, pouting, childish prettiness, but with all love and belief in love departed from it—the sadder for its beauty, like that wondrous Medusa-face, with the passionate, passionless lips."

"HIGHGATE CEMETERY"

In a letter to Robert Bridges dated 28 October 1886, Gerard Manley Hopkins wrote: "How admirable are Blackmore and Hardy! Their merits are much eclipsed by the overdone reputation of the Evans–Eliot–Cross woman (poor creature! one ought not to speak slightingly, I know), half real power, half imposition. . . ." (*Selected Prose*, edited by Gerald Roberts, Oxford University Press, 1980, p. 148.)

"MARGARET FULLER, 1847"

From *Memoirs of Margaret Fuller Ossoli*, quoted by Paula Blanchard in *Margaret Fuller: From Transcendentalism to Revolution* (Delta/Seymour Lawrence, 1979, p. 167): "Once I was almost all intellect; now I am almost all feeling. Nature vindicates her rights, and I feel all Italy glowing beneath the Saxon crust. This cannot last long; I shall burn to ashes if all this smoulders here much longer. I must die if I do not burst forth in genius or heroism."

"GRASMERE"

Whatever may be conjectured about the attachment between Dorothy Wordsworth and her brother William—and there has been much conjecture, most recently by Robert Gittings and Jo Manton in *Dorothy Wordsworth* (Oxford, 1985)—the undisputed circumstances are that they were born a year apart, were separated at the age of seven and eight respectively and saw little of one another until they were in their teens; that once reunited, they lived together, with brief separations, from 1794 until William's death in 1850 (Dorothy, although for many years incapacitated, survived him by five years); that during a stay in France, William fell in love with Annette Vallon, by whom in 1792 he had a daughter, Caroline; and that in 1802 William married Dorothy's longtime friend Mary Hutchinson, by whom he had five more children— John, Dorothy, Thomas, Catharine, and William, Jr. From December 1799 until the spring of 1808, the Wordsworths made their home at Grasmere, in what is now known as Dove Cottage; here, at various times, Samuel Taylor Coleridge, and later Thomas De Quincey, were part of the household. In 1813, after living briefly at two other houses in Grasmere itself, the family moved to Rydal Mount, where Dorothy, William, and Mary would all reside for the rest of their lives.

"COLEORTON"

"Wordsworth . . . has been described," wrote Douglas Bush in *Mythology and the Romantic Tradition in English Poetry* (Harvard University Press, 1969, p. 51), "as Coleridge's greatest work, and, like all his other works, left unfinished."

From the letters of Dorothy Wordsworth, as quoted in Gittings and Manton, pp. 155ff.: "We are crammed in our little nest edge full as you will suppose. . . . Every bed lodges two persons at present." (January 1806) "Our continuing here during another winter would be attended with so many serious inconveniences, especially to my Brother, who has no quiet corner in which to pursue his studies, no room but that where we all sit (to say nothing of the unwholesomeness of these low small rooms for such a number of persons). . . . We think of going into Leicestershire, Sir George B[eaumont] having offered us their house for the winter." (June 1806)

The images of the woman with the pince-nez, the crouching mother, and the overturned baby carriage occur in a sequence from the Sergei Eisenstein film *Potemkin*, depicting an incident during the uprising of 1905, when Russian government troops advanced against unarmed civilians on the steps above the harbor at Odessa.

"AN ANATOMY OF MIGRAINE"

From Thomas De Quincey, *Confessions of an English Opium-Eater* (Oxford University Press, 1985, p. 76): "The dream commenced with a music which now I often heard in dreams—a music of preparation and of awakening suspense; a music like the opening of the Coronation Anthem, and which, like *that*, gave the feeling of a vast march—of infinite cavalcades filing off—and the tread of innumerable armies."

From Simone Weil, *Gravity and Grace* (G. P. Putnam's Sons, 1952, pp. 7, 73–74): "Nothing in the world can rob us of the power to say 'I.' Nothing except extreme affliction. Nothing is worse than extreme affliction which destroys the 'I' from outside, because after that we can no longer destroy it ourselves. What happens to those whose 'I' has been destroyed from outside by affliction? It is not possible to imagine anything for them but annihilation according to the atheistic or materialistic conception.

"Though they may have lost their 'I,' it does not mean that they have no more egoism. Quite the reverse. . . . Human injustice as a general rule produces not martyrs but quasi-damned souls. Beings who have fallen into this quasi-hell are like someone stripped and wounded by robbers. They have lost the clothing of character."

From Henry James, *The Wings of the Dove*, Book First (Modern Library Edition, 1930, pp. 36, 37): ". . . all intercourse with her sister had the effect of casting down her courage and tying her hands, adding daily to her sense of the part, not always either uplifting or sweetening, that the bond of blood might play in one's life. . . . Bereaved, disappointed, demoralized, querulous, she was all the more sharply and insistently Kate's elder and Kate's own. . . . She [Kate] noticed with profundity that disappointment made people selfish. . . ."

From *The Brain: Mystery of Matter and Mind* (U.S. News Books, 1981, p. 23): "Brain surgeon Roger Sperry of the California Institute of Technology concluded that the brain's consciousness encompassed and transcended its physical workings: 'In the human head there are forces within forces within forces, as in no other cubic half-foot of the universe that we know.' "

Again, from Simone Weil in *Gravity and Grace*, p. 133: "Time bears the thinking being in spite of himself toward that which he cannot bear, and which will come all the same."

From a note by Martin Gardner to *The Annotated Alice* (Bramhall House, 1960, p. 231): "Tweedledum and Tweedledee are what geometers call 'enantiomorphs,' mirror-image forms of each other. That Carroll intended this is strongly suggested by Tweedledee's favorite word, 'contrariwise,' and by the fact that they extend right and left hands for a handshake. Tenniel's picture of the two enantiomorphs arrayed for battle, standing in identical postures, indicates that he looked upon the twins in the same way. . . ."

chī-as′ma, n.; pl. chī-as′mà·tà. [Gr. *chiasma*, two lines crossed, from *chiazein*, to mark with the Greek letter chi.]
  1. in anatomy, a crossing or intersection of the optic nerves on the ventral surface of the brain.
  2. any crosswise fusion.
chī-as′mus, n.; pl. chī-as′mi. [Mod. L.: Gr. *chiasmos*, placing crosswise.] an inversion of the second of two parallel phrases, clauses, etc.; as, do not live to eat, but eat to live.

—Webster's Unabridged Dictionary

From *The Diary of Virginia Woolf*, edited by Anne Olivier Bell (Harcourt Brace Jovanovich, 1977–84): ". . . Often down here I have entered into a sanctuary; a nunnery; had a religious retreat; of great agony once; & always some terror: so afraid one is of loneliness: of seeing to the bottom of the vessel. That is one of the experiences I have had here in some Augusts; & got then to a consciousness of what I call 'reality': a thing I see before me, something abstract; but residing in the downs or sky; beside which nothing matters; in which I shall rest & continue to exist. Reality I call it. And I fancy sometimes this is the most necessary thing to me: that which I seek. But who knows—once one takes a pen & writes? . . ." (Monday 10 September 1928; Volume Three, p. 196.)

"I've had some very curious visions in this room too, lying in bed, mad, & seeing the sunlight quivering like gold water, on the wall. I've heard the voices of the dead here. And felt, through it all, exquisitely happy." (Wednesday 9 January 1924; Volume Two, p. 283.)

"MAN FEEDING PIGEONS"

From the *Paradiso* of Dante Alighieri, Canto XXX:

> E se l'infimo grado in sè raccoglie
>   sì grande lume, quant' è la larghezza
>   di questo rosa nell' estreme foglie?
>
> (And if the lowest step gathereth so large
>   a light within itself, what then the amplitude
>   of the rose's outmost petals?)
>
>   —Translation by Philip H. Wicksteed

ACKNOWLEDGMENTS

Grateful acknowledgment is due to the following periodicals, in which the poems that make up this collection (a few with different phrasing) first appeared: *Albatross*: "Progress at Building Site with (Fewer) Pigeons"; *Cream City Review*: "Continental Drift"; *Grand Forks Audubon Society Newsletter*: "The Waterfall"; *Grand Street*: "Babel Aboard the Hellas International Express," "Coleorton," "Medusa at Broadstairs," "Saloniki"; *Ironwood*: "The Nereids of Seriphos," "Seriphos Unvisited"; *The Kenyon Review*: "Olympia"; *The New Republic*: "Alice"; *The New Yorker*: "An Anatomy of Migraine," "George Eliot Country," "A Hermit Thrush," "Highgate Cemetery" (under the title "At the Grave of George Eliot"), "Hippocrene," "Man Feeding Pigeons," "Margaret Fuller, 1847," "The Olive Groves of Thasos," "Venice Revisited"; *North Dakota Quarterly*: "Perseus Airborne"; *Observer*, London: "London Inside and Outside"; *Oxford Poetry*: "Runes, Blurs, Sap Rising"; *Parnassus*: "Atlas Immobilized"; *The Paris Review*: "Grasmere," "Rydal Mount"; *Poetry*: "Athena," "Dodona: Asked of the Oracle," "Leaving Yánnina," "Medusa," "Perseus," "Thermopylae"; *Southwest Review*: "Tempe in the Rain"; *2PLUS2*: "Ano Prinios," "Archaic Figure"; *William and Mary Review*: "Tidewater Winter"; *The Yale Review*: "The Odessa Steps." "George Eliot Country" was reprinted in *The George Eliot Fellowship Review*, 1985. "Grasmere" was reprinted in *The Pushcart Prize*, X, 1985. "Midsummer in the Blueberry Barrens" first appeared in *The Summer Solstice*, published by the Sarabande Press, 1983.

For financial support, and for space and leisure to write in, the author is greatly indebted to the Academy of American Poets, the American Academy and Institute of Arts and Letters, The College of William and Mary, the Corporation of Yaddo, the Djerassi Foundation, and the John Simon Guggenheim Foundation.

A NOTE ABOUT THE AUTHOR

Amy Clampitt was born and brought up in New Providence, Iowa, graduated from Grinnell College, and has since lived mainly in New York City. Her poems began appearing in *The New Yorker* in 1978, and have since been widely published in magazines and literary journals. Her first full-length collection, *The Kingfisher*, published in 1983, was followed in 1985 by *What the Light Was Like*. She is currently Visiting Writer at Amherst College.

A NOTE ON THE TYPE

The text of this book was set on the Linotype in Fair-field, a typeface designed by the distinguished American artist and engraver Rudolph Ruzicka (1883–1978). Fairfield displays the sober and sane qualities of a master craftsman whose talent has long been dedicated to clarity. Rudolph Ruzicka was born in Bohemia and came to America in 1894. He designed and illustrated many books and was the creator of a considerable list of individual prints in a variety of techniques.

Composed by Heritage Printers, Inc.,
Charlotte, North Carolina

Printed and bound by Halliday Lithographers,
West Hanover, Massachusetts

Typography and binding design
by Dorothy Schmiderer